Letting in the Rumour

Poetry by Gillian Clarke

The Sundial
Letter from a Far Country
Selected Poems

Gillian Clarke

Letting in the Rumour

CARCANET

for my mother

and for my late father
John Penri Williams

Acknowledgements are due to the editors of the following magazines, periodicals, anthologies and programmes: PBS Anthologies 1986-7; 1988-9; *The New Welsh Review; PN Review; The New England Review* and *Bread Loaf Quarterly; The Poetry of Pembrokeshire* (Seren Books); *The Poetry of Snowdonia* (Seren Books); *Poetry Wales; Planet; Gown* (Belfast); *The Belfast Review; Glas Nos* (CND Cymru); *Singing Brink* (Arvon Press); *Neighbours* (Peterloo); *PEN New Poetry 11; With a Poet's Eye* (Tate Gallery); *There's a Poet Behind You* (A & C Black); BBC World Service; where some of these poems first appeared. The author also acknowledges the Welsh Arts Council for a bursary received in 1981, when her research on *Cofiant* began.

First published in 1989 by
Carcanet Press Limited
208-212 Corn Exchange Buildings
Manchester M4 3BQ UK

British Library Cataloguing in Publication Data

Clarke, Gillian
  Letting in the rumour
  I. Title
  821'. 914

  ISBN O-85635-757-X

The publisher acknowledges financial assistance from
the Arts Council of Great Britain.

Typeset in 10pt Palatino by Bryan Williamson, Manchester
Printed in England by SRP Ltd., Exeter

Contents

At One Thousand Feet

Nobody comes but the postman
and the farmer with winter fodder.

A-road and motorway avoid me.
The national grid has left me out.

For power I catch wind.
In my garden clear water rises.

A wind spinning the blades
of the mill to blinding silver

lets in the rumour,
grief on the radio.

America telephones.
A postcard comes from Poland.

In the sling of its speed the comet
flowers to perihelion over the chimney.

I hold the sky to my ear to hear
pandemonium whispering.

Neighbours

That spring was late. We watched the sky
and studied charts for shouldering isobars.
Birds were late to pair. Crows drank from the lamb's eye.

Over Finland small birds fell: song-thrushes
steering north, smudged signatures on light,
migrating warblers, nightingales.

Wing-beats failed over fjords, each lung a sip of gall.
Children were warned of their dangerous beauty.
Milk was spilt in Poland. Each quarrel

the blowback from some old story,
a mouthful of bitter air from the Ukraine
brought by the wind out of its box of sorrows.

This spring a lamb sips caesium on a Welsh hill.
A child, lifting her face to drink the rain,
takes into her blood the poisoned arrow.

Now we are all neighbourly, each little town
in Europe twinned to Chernobyl, each heart
with the burnt fireman, the child on the Moscow train.

In the democracy of the virus and the toxin
we wait. We watch for bird migrations,
one bird returning with green in its voice,

glasnost,
golau glas,
a first break of blue.

golau glas blue light

8

Windmill

On the stillest day
not enough breath to rock the hedge
it smashes the low sun to smithereens.

Quicker than branch to find a thread of air
that'll tow a gale off the Atlantic
by way of Lundy, Irish Sea.

At night it knocks stars from their perches
and casts a rhythmic beating of the moon
into my room in bright blades.

It kneels into the wind-race
and slaps black air to foam.
Helping to lower and lift it again

I feel it thrash in dark water
drumming with winds from the Americas
to run through my fingers' circle

holding the earth's breath.

Listening for Trains

I.

All day gale-warnings.
Hard to believe when air hangs

wet in the plum-trees. High
above their crowns the first sigh

touches the windmill's blades
to a blurred cloud

of wings. Then the sound
of the sea mounting the land

and the storm's engine begins.
Deep inland gardens

lap quiet as pools
under the air and nothing spills

or rustles. Out here
I'm the one with my ear

to the line,
listening for trains.

II.

Sunburnt children in baggy shorts,
Clark's sandals, cotton frocks,

gathering berries in green
backwaters through tangled vine

of woodbine, filbert and bramble.
And the day-long scramble

where the first cool touch
of hands is chance, and that brush

of another's saltiness. Underfoot
the sleepers are hot

and the parted tracks run free
until they merge above the sea

beyond the farm, the distant mill.
My heart beats against the steel

a gathering power that is mine
until I hear the train drumming the line.

Storm

The cat lies low, too scared
to cross the garden.

For two days we are bowed
by a whiplash of hurricane.

The hill's a wind-harp.
Our bones are flutes of ice.

The heart drums in its small room
and the river rattles its pebbles.

Thistlefields are comb and paper
whisperings of syllable and bone

till no word's left
but thud and rumble of

something with hooves or wheels,
something breathing too hard.

Seal

When the milk-arrow stabs she comes
water-fluent down the long green miles.
Her milk leaks into the sea, blue
blossoming in an opal.

The pup lies patient in his cot of stone.
They meet with cries, caress as people do.
She lies down for his suckling, lifts him
with a flipper from the sea's reach
when the tide fills his throat with salt.

This is the fourteenth day. In two days
no bitch-head will break the brilliance
listening for baby-cries.
Down in the thunder of that other country
the bulls are calling and her uterus is empty.

Alone and hungering in his fallen shawl
he'll nuzzle the Atlantic and be gone.
If that day's still his moult will lie
a gleaming ring on sand
like the noose she slips on the sea.

Ichthyosaur
at the exhibition of Dinosaurs from China

Jurassic travellers
trailing a wake of ammonites.
Vertebrae swirl in stone's currents,
the broken flotilla of a pilgrimage.
Bone-pods open their secret marrow.

Behind glass she dies, birth-giving.
Millions of years too late it can still move us,
the dolphin-flip of her spine
and the frozen baby turning its head
to the world at the last moment
as all our babies do, facing the storm
of drowning as it learned to live.

Small obstetric tragedy,
like the death of a lamb at a field-edge
the wrong way up or strangled at birth
by the mothering cord.
Perhaps earth heaved, slapped a burning hand
on both of them as he ducked under her lintel,
leaving only a grace of bones
eloquent as a word in stone.

Cold Knap Lake

We once watched a crowd
pull a drowned child from the lake.
Blue-lipped and dressed in water's long green silk
she lay for dead.

Then kneeling on the earth,
a heroine, her red head bowed,
her wartime cotton frock soaked,
my mother gave a stranger's child her breath.
The crowd stood silent,
drawn by the dread of it.

The child breathed, bleating
and rosy in my mother's hands.
My father took her home to a poor house
and watched her thrashed for almost drowning.

Was I there?
Or is that troubled surface something else
shadowy under the dipped fingers of willows
where satiny mud blooms in cloudiness
after the treading, heavy webs of swans
as their wings beat and whistle on the air?

All lost things lie under closing water
in that lake with the poor man's daughter.

Apples

They fill with heat, dewfall, a night of rain.
In a week they have reddened, the seed gone black
in each star-heart. Soft thud of fruit
in the deepening heat of the day.
Out of the delicate petals of secret skin
and that irreversible moment when the fruit set,
such a hard harvest, so cold and sharp on the tongue.

They look up from the grass, too many to save.
A lapful of windfalls with worms in their hearts,
under my thumb the pulse of original sin,
flesh going brown as the skin curls over my knife.
I drown them in water and wine, pushing them under,
then breathe apples simmering in sugar and spice,
fermenting under the tree in sacs of juice
so swollen they'd burst under a wasp's foot.

Oranges

So many of them among the stones,
each like a float over a lobster pot
coming in numerous as the drowned.

Up early at the Little Harbour,
we found the treasure we'd sought
all the Saturdays of childhood.
First gold brought generously
to a mean Britain. I remember
the water calm as milk licking
the sand with little oily tongues.

We filled our sleeves,
gathered our skirts to make sacks,
bumped uncomfortably homeward.
Crates like the smashed ribcages of sheep.
Across milky water the wreck
was languorous, her tilted deck
rolling with Atalanta's gold.

Salt at first bite, then bitter pith
and a sharp juice. My tongue searched
for the cloying concentrate I knew
or the scent the miner spoke of,
an orange broken at snap-time underground
breathed a mile away
if the wind's in the right direction.

Fires on Llŷn

At sunset we climb Uwchmynydd
to a land's end
where R.S. Thomas walks, finding
the footprint of God
warm in the shoe of the hare.

Words shape-shift to wind,
a flight of oystercatchers,
whinchat on a bush,
two cormorants fast-dipping wings
in a brilliant sea.

Over the holy sound
Enlli is dark in a ruff
of foam. Any pebble or shell
might be the knuckle-bone
or vertebra of a saint.

Three English boys throw stones.
Choughs sound alarm.
Sea-birds rise and twenty thousand saints
finger the shingle
to the sea's intonation.

Facing west, we've talked for hours
of our history,
thinking of Ireland
and the hurt cities,
gunshot on lonely farms,

praised unsectarian saints,
Enlli open
to the broken rosary
of their coracles,
praying in Latin and Welsh.

Done with cliff-talking
we turn inland, thinking
of home silently filling
with shadows, the hearth
quiet for the struck match,

our bed spread with clean sheets.
Our eyes are tired
with sun-gazing. Suddenly
we shout – the farms burn.
Through binoculars we see

distant windows curtained with flame.
The fires are real
that minute while we gasp,
begin to run, then realise
windows catch, not fire but

the setting sun. We are struck still
without a word
in any language. See the hares run,
windows darken,
hear the sea's mumbled novenas.

Talking of Burnings
in Walter Savage Landor's Smithy

The house eases awake to the tick
of clocks, water burbling
in the complexity of drains.
We make slow fires, smoke straight
as a cat's tail against larchwoods.
The Honddu plaits its waters in the rising sun.

Uphill the poet's house lies broken
in a memory of flame.
Face of a stranger in a holy window.
An abbey sacked and word on word
of a monk's patient flamboyance
gilds for a moment and is gone.

Cromwell fires the map.
Peasants come with roaring torches.
A terrorist's bomb.
Another falling wall.
Under the rubble a young girl's voice
blurs to silence as she lets go.

Through house and church and priory
of a tenanted land
the long fires burn, fronds
curling through the heartwood
of great houses prising stone from stone
in two thousand years of burnings.

With petrol and a match
the ridge-beam goes and the roof sags
like the saddleback of a broken mare.
The displaced leave with their burden,
smoke pressed between scorched sheets,
and all the bridges down.

Border

It crumbles
where the land forgets its name
and I'm foreign in my own country.
Fallow, pasture, ploughland
ripped from the hill
beside a broken farm.

The word's exactness
slips from children's tongues.
Saints fade in the parishes.
Fields blur between the scar
of hedgerow and new road.
History forgets itself.

At the garage they're polite.
"Sorry love, no Welsh."
At the shop I am slapped
by her hard "What!"
They came for the beauty
but could not hear it speak.

Poetry Class

In the classroom in Grangetown
we have been listening to water.

The river rustles in its limestone tent.
The ramskull brims with winter rain.

The whirlpool flickers
in the ammonite's eye.

A village drowns
in a reservoir

tethered to hills
by the dipping rope of a lane.

In their sleep these children of India,
Somalia, Bangladesh, Wales,

will dream of the Mellte
they have never seen

streaming out of the cave-mouth
into the snows of morning.

Post Script

Epiphany – and burning of the poems
with clippings of the hedge we laid last week,
long loops of bramble, cherry, wild laburnum,
old summer leaves and sodden autumn smoke.

All afternoon I put them to the fire,
handfuls of poems turned to scrolls of vellum,
each a small chimney for a twist of air
then from each broken throat a gasp of flame.

The pages lapse and gild before they burn
like a First Folio lying in a chest.
There's splendour there (both spellings) dew and dawn,
love and philosophy and loss and lust.

Some of your poems had no voice at all
but sing now with a little sigh of death.
You would be glad to see the way your words
are turned to incense on the fire's breath.

Now they are famous on the hill for miles
and take the green wood by the throat in rage,
ode, elegy, sestina, vilanelle
scare as they couldn't, too docile on the page.

The rotten core of mulch is torn apart
by the stoat-teeth of your verses, now alive.
Your scansion and your imagery start
a sting of sweetness in the bonfire's hive.

Each page committed. Your last poems burn.
Out with the cliché, archaism, weed.
They drift the hill and my mind's clean again.
New year and a fired language is what we need.

Marged

I think of her sometimes when I lie in bed,
falling asleep in the room I have made in the roof-space
over the old dark parlŵr where she died
alone in winter, ill and penniless.
Lighting the lamps, November afternoons,
a reading book, whisky gold in my glass.
At my type-writer tapping under stars
at my new roof-window, radio tunes
and dog for company. Or parking the car
where through the mud she called her single cow
up from the field, under the sycamore.
Or looking at the hills she looked at too.
I find her broken crocks, digging her garden.
What else do we share, but being women?

On her Windowsill

A lantern of sour soil
where ferns and mosses
stood still all winter
and put down fibres as likely to root
as bones under the long
broken light of cathedrals.

Maidenhair, each heart-leaf
withered on its wire.
In the petrified forest
one stem straightens
under a tender bead of green.

Syngonium. Geranium.
All winter they pressed
withered faces to the panes
watching the empty lane.
They shrank from day to day
not dreaming of a future
where bright vans would turn the corner
and the lane lead everywhere.

A curlew skull,
pair of blue blades,
sand running out between them,
that song of elegy and celebration
smashed in its box of bone.
On Aberffraw beach I broke its throat,
derelict bird,
beak blue as mussel shells
in which you hear spring
lament over estuaries.

Bottles, plugs of soil
washed from their throats.
Lotions and linctus in coloured glass,
rennet in stone.
Fluids that set junkets
or eased the influenza or croup
until the last time when she filled
her throat with earth and could not wake.

This week, turning soil
to plant the silver birch
the hawthorn and the rowan,
we find shards of rose on white,
a rim, a curve, a leaf.
Out of brokenness
I fit together her spilled cup.

Housewife

After weeks of travelling I tend fires,
wipe dust as a spatula takes cream,
crumble bread for birds in the slate house
in the plum tree, scatter pellets over water.
A fish rises, red sun in its mirror.
Iris and rush lift blades out of frayed ribbons
and lily leaves lie among shivering verticals.

Rain and wind have overturned the crocus,
unblocked wall-crannies. The spring rises.
The windmill spins. They have not missed me.
With a warm cloth I clear hills,
a tractor ploughing, farms, fields whose names
I know. In their bracelets of hot water
my wrists root.

Overheard in County Sligo

I married a man from County Roscommon
and I live at the back of beyond
with a field of cows and a yard of hens
and six white geese on the pond.

At my door's a square of yellow corn
caught up by its corners and shaken,
and the road runs down through the open gate
and freedom's there for the taking.

I had thought to work on the Abbey stage
or have my name in a book,
to see my thought on the printed page,
or still the crowd with a look.

But I turn to fold the breakfast cloth
and to polish the lustre and brass,
to order and dust the tumbled rooms
and find my face in the glass.

I ought to feel I'm a happy woman
for I lie in the lap of the land,
and I married a man from County Roscommon
and I live at the back of beyond.

Shawl

Mamgu, a century old, loops coloured wool.
She can't see them now. The shawl

is in her mind. She touches colour.
Her fingers fly as bats at dusk in summer,

bringing the dark. The shawl grows over her knees
heavy as shadows lengthening under trees.

Her fingers write on air. She talks, walking
the old roads, tarmac'ed now, but in her mind

bone-white, scuffed by the boots of girls trailing
their hems in dust. She takes each bend,

each hill, gives every field its name.
Her hands cross-hatch the air. Garden and room

are gradually shadowed, her psalms'
memorial litany, a list of farms.

My Box

My box is made of golden oak,
my lover's gift to me.
He fitted hinges and a lock
of brass and a bright key.
He made it out of winter nights,
sanded and oiled and planed,
engraved inside the heavy lid
in brass, a golden tree.

In my box are twelve black books
where I have written down
how we have sanded, oiled and planed,
planted a garden, built a wall,
seen jays and goldcrests, rare red kites,
found the wild heartsease, drilled a well,
harvested apples and words and days
and planted a golden tree.

On an open shelf I keep my box.
Its key is in the lock.
I leave it there for you to read,
or them, when we are dead,
how everything is slowly made,
how slowly things made me,
a tree, a lover, words, a box,
books and a golden tree.

Falling

Soft slip of the loft-ladder's feet
on worn carpet. It went
under my foot on the first step
as land shelving from the littoral to the deep.

I can swim, and for a moment,
elbows on the beam over the kitchen,
I swung like a toy on a table-edge, thinking
he would catch me, free-falling.

Time slowed
as the boat of the room capsized
and I fell
till the stone floor slammed –

– while he had time
for the heart's crash and bones' brokenness,
the body like a bowl in pieces,
silence lengthening after me simple as linen.

Falling's a trust game. Fall simply
like a baby, nothing breaks.
He soothes my bruises with ointments,
brings grapes in a brown bag, his eyes

loving and sorry at the open door.
At night the soft slip of the loft-ladder
wakes me and I weep.
'You're safe now' he says, 'Sleep.'

I drop through darkness to be slammed awake
and always he is there, with healing.

Dream

Suddenly waking at five
plunged wholly into the catastrophe
I lay at the edge of the dark
where the brilliance is.
Slowly I knew I was awake
among the ruins.

Only walking the path
in my blue dressing-gown,
seeing bright breath where the river is,
the house calm and white in the rising sun,
a glittering loop of swifts about the barn,
could I believe the world unbroken.

The blackbird who sang yesterday
and the day before
calls from the chimney still
'this is all mine..all mine..all mine'

Roadblock

Over and over these nights I dream of horses.
Sometimes I'm walking the known lane home
to find them standing, immovable giants
blocking my way. No creak of brass or harness.
No stamping hoof. Bronze beasts in a museum,
gold flanks flowing in a still compliance,
each head curved over another's neck,
and past the mass of them the house-lights gleaming.
I remember beautiful boys on the road from school
shouldering courage between them, beast in check
but only just, and my heart beating
too fast for love and fear of them. In the cool
dawn I'm stark awake. You're dead to the world
blocking my way to somewhere with your sleeping gold.

Looking

Kate in full day in the heat of the sun
looks into the grave, sees in that unearthing
of a Roman settlement, under a stone
only the shadow of a skeleton.

Gwyn on his back in the dark, lying
on the lawn dry from months of drought,
finds in the sky through the telescope
the fuzzy dust of stars he has been searching.

Imprint of bones is a constellation
shining against silence, against darkness,
and stars are the pearly vertebrae
of water-drops against the drought, pelvis,

skull, scapula five million light years old
wink in the glass, and stardust is all we hold
of the Roman lady's negative
in the infinite dark of the grave.

Binary
for Owain

You take blue plums from a bowl.
"Think only of two. Each answer's yes or no."

Negative. Positive. Light flickers in my mind
coming and going in uncertainty,
doubt's dark nebula against a galaxy.

In old films held to light
you are new-born, small child,
and we count fingers and toes.
The little pig squeals all the way home.
We count stairs to ease the way to bed,
trees, gates, lamp-posts on a long walk.

The bloom of blue plums holds your fingerprint.
"You do it now. Each plum is two."

It should be easier than fingers.
Pairs mean more. Couples. Parents.
Mother and child. The body's symmetry.
I move a plum, think multiples of two.
I have it. The answer's right.
You're pleased with both of us.

In the cold sky I show you Jupiter,
its Galilean moons, the nebula
that rears its head before Orion's sword,
and Algol, blue dwarf and yellow giant
true binary star that calculates the dark
and counts its little day in the wink of an eye.

You teach me binary and distant coda
deep in the dark tracks of songs you make,
uncountable chords like Saturn's echoing rings.
I listen, counting sound,
wild poetry you sing to your guitar.
Your brother drums.
I think I understand.

Snakeskin

for Michael and Adam Horovitz

Trace of a snail
that writes a lover's name;
first track of the morning
the dog makes in long wet grass;
a water-snake of light
at turn of tide;
shed private silk
on a bedroom carpet.

That other grass-snake, ammonite
and looking with hard eye, tongue
a little flame in Frances' Cotswold garden.
A slide of light, softly
it oiled away, a rearrangement
of silvers and greens, too deep
in blackthorn to be reached.

Shed images of snake
and nothing, now,
her dresses given away,
but an impression in grass.

The Hare

i.m. Frances Horovitz 1938-1983

That March night I remember how we heard
a baby crying in a neighbouring room
but found him sleeping quietly in his cot.

The others went to bed and we sat late
talking of children and the men we loved.
You thought you'd like another child. 'Too late.'

you said. And we fell silent, thought a while
of yours with his copper hair and mine,
a grown daughter and sons.

Then, that joke we shared, our phases of the moon.
'Sisterly lunacy' I said. You liked
the phrase. It became ours. Different

as earth and air, yet in one trace that week
we towed the calends like boats reining
the oceans of the world at the full moon.

Suddenly from the fields we heard again
a baby cry, and standing at the door
listened for minutes, eyes and ears soon used

to the night. It was cold. In the east
the river made a breath of shining sound.
The cattle in the field were shadow black.

A cow coughed. Some slept, and some pulled grass.
I could smell blossom from the blackthorn
and see their thorny crowns against the sky.

And then again, a sharp cry from the hill.
'A hare' we said together, not speaking
of fox or trap that held it in a lock

of terrible darkness. Both admitted
next day to lying guilty hours awake
at the crying of the hare. You told me

of sleeping at last in the jaws of a bad dream.
I saw all the suffering of the world
in a single moment. Then I heard

a voice say 'But this is nothing, nothing
to the mental pain'. I couldn't speak of it.
I thought about your dream as you lay ill.

In the last heavy nights before full moon,
when its face seems sorrowful and broken,
I look through binoculars. Its seas flower

like cloud over water, it wears its craters
like silver rings. Even in dying you
menstruated as a woman in health

considering to have a child or no.
When they hand me insults or little hurts
and I'm on fire with my arguments

at your great distance you can calm me still.
Your dream, my sleeplessness, the cattle
asleep under a full moon,

and out there
the dumb and stiffening body of the hare.

Hare in July

All spring and summer the bitch has courted the hare,
thrilled to the scent in a gateway, the musk of speed.
Months while I dug and planted and watched a mist
of green grow to a dense foliage,
neat rows in a scaffolding of sticks and nets,
nose down, tail up in thickening grass
she has been hunting the hare.

Today the big machines are in the field
raising their cromlechs against the sun.
The garden is glamorous with summer.
We cut and rake grass for the fire.
She leaps the bank bearing the weight of her gift,
the golden body of a young jack hare,
blood in its nostrils and a drowning sound.

'Drop' we say 'drop'. Heartbeat running out,
its eyes as wide and black as peaty lakes.
I feel under my finger one snapped rib
fine as a needle in a punctured lung
where it leaped too wild against the bitch's jaw.
Light fades from its fur, and in its eyes
a sudden fall of snow.

Trophy

'Thorpe Satchville Beagles, 3 hours, Clawson, January 26th 1928'

In the ice-trap of January
trees splinter a low sun
and the pond's brilliance
is glazed to pearl like the eye
of the old blind dog.

Hares start from furrows
to fire the land, their ears
small standing shadows, each bone
an instrument for listening,
each foot on the pulse of the earth.

Musk in the brain, the hounds
are a parliament of braying.
Of all creatures the hare
has the largest heart,
his blood-volume the greatest.

This one outran the pack
for a hare's nine lives,
and does again through an afternoon
when trees sing in ice, and air
is opal for three winter hours.

I heard of a hare who outran hounds
for a day and died of heartburst, found
at his death-moment, his arteries
full of air-bubbles instead of blood.
Or hares on aerodrome runways racing jets.

When they cast the torn body away
and saved the golden head
for the taxidermist's shield,
in turn they emptied the horn
in The Star, Long Clawson.

At Thorpe Satchville the kennelman
set bowls before his pets,
and rubbed their coats
to their usual shining.

The Rothko Room

He crushed charcoal with a city's rubies,
saw such visions of soft-edged night and day
as stop the ears with silence. In this,
the last room after hours in the gallery,
a mesh diffuses London's light and sound.
The Indian keeper nods to sleep, marooned
in a trapezium of black on red.

We few who stop are quiet as if we prayed
in this room after Turner's turbulence.
Coming and going through paint's water-curtains
turning a corner suddenly we find
a city burns, a cathedral comes down
with a last blaze filling its gaudy lantern
and windows buckle as a tenement falls.

Rack the heart for memory or sense
and reds like these come crowding out of dream:
musk mallow, goat's rue, impatiens,
loosestrife, hellebore, belladonna, nightshade,
poppysilks crushed in their velvety soot,
and digitalis purpurea, red on maroon,
drop dappled gloves along an August lane.

A morning's laundry marking glass with steam
on rainy Mondays where a blackbird sings
sodden in dripping dark-red lilac trees.
We look, myopic, down his corridors
through misted spectacles of broken glass
window on window, scaffolding of pain
red on maroon and black, black on maroon.

Red Poppy
from a painting by Georgia O'Keefe

"The meaning of a word
is not as exact
as the meaning of a colour"

So she walks out of the rectangles
of hard, crowded America
and floods the skies over southern plains

with carmine, scarlet,
with the swirl of poppy-silk.
There is music in it, and drumbeat.

You can put out the sun with poppy,
lie in long grass with beetle and ladybird
and shade your eyes with its awnings,

its heart of charcoal.
Wine glasses held to candles
or your veined lids against the sun.

The waters open for a million years,
petal after petal in the thundering river,
stamens of flying spray at its whirlpool heart.

Red mountain where the light slides
through the beating red of every Texan dusk,
and dark earth opens in a sooty yawn.

She paints out language, land, sky,
so we can only look and drown in deeps
of poppy under a thundering sun.

Physalis

Year after year
I've tried to grow them.
October lanterns

in the wasting garden,
whispery rattle
of the hardening year.

They brazen out the dark,
flamboyance initialling
the white page.

Months while we hug fires,
stamp like horses
in our haloes of breath,

and the pond's shut hard
on the gleam of fish,
these fire her house

hanging their heads among
honesty's mother-of-pearl
at winter's blurred mirror.

February

Lamb-grief in the fields
and a cold as hard as slate.
Foot and hoof are shod

with ice. Our footprints
seem as old as ferns in stone.
Air rings in ash and thorn.

Ice on the rain-butt, thick
as a shield and the tap chokes,
its thumb in its throat.

The stream runs black
in a ruff of ice, its caught breath
furls a frieze of air.

At night ice sings
to the strum of my thrown stones
like a snapped harp-string.

The pond's glass eye holds
leaf, reed, fish, paperweight
in a dream of stone

Lamb

Cart-track and hill
and a wall of river-boulders.

Hail-stones are sharp
in a glance of sunlight.

At the gate she stops me,
nervous and watching

but too late to run.
She is there in her blood.

I am stone. I am gatepost.
The lamb comes easily

under her bridge of bone
as the stream from its ice.

He is safe in his halo
staggering in brilliance.

Blood gleams on my boot.

Gannet

hangs on the wind on motionless wings
and falls a hundred feet

on a gleam of fish.
The sea gasps

as the hiss of iron
in the farrier's bucket.

The black wave,
a white-hot knife of light,

sea's retina dazzled
by the sign of the cross.

Night Flying

We fall to earth like children playing war.
Low-flying jets by night,
their roar out of dark breaks sleep.
Attack comes from behind, blindfolding us.
It's not like playing but remembering war,
crouching under the stairs for the all-clear.

They see through our uncurtained windows
as we turn to each other in the dark.
They search the fields with their night eye
for creatures crossing no-man's-land,
a sniper on a branch, a hare
with the moon in its eye, a terrorist
taking the ditch way home, white faces
at windows of lonely farms.

Who knows what outrages we'd be plotting
in bedroom and burrow and hollow oak,
what subterfuge we'd be dreaming, what outbreak
of peace, what tender subversions as we cry
in each other's arms at such an outrage
as their shadows cross the moonlit garden,
quartering the privacy of dreams.

In January

A day of wings – jet from Aberporth,
glittering dragonfly
towing its shadow from the south
over a yellow hill. It breaks the day.

Ice beneath the dog's paw cries
in the silence we're left with. A pair
of buzzards circle in bright air
slowly over an oakwood, and three crows

come up for air from a frozen field.
Over the brow, where the lane falls
into sheer light, air is filled
with clouds of glassy insect wings.

The cities can forget on days like this
all the world's wars. It's we
out on the open hill who see
the day crack under the shadow of the cross.

Tory Party Conference, Bournemouth, 1986
for Bill Davies

While Bill was dancing on his window-sill
to a song called 'Up on the Roof'
the police were mounting the stairs.

He rocked the town with his eye,
tilted the streets and rooftops,
rolling the warships in the Channel.

Da Vinci's proportioned man
his limbs outreaching
for the perfect circle.

The town trembled in the glass
as he pirouetted on his little stage
till the police broke down the door.

Then he learned how for minutes he'd danced
in the sights of the marksman's gun,
his fingers and feet describing

the cold ring of its eye.

Times like These

Too heavy-hearted to go walking
in beech-woods. At night the children's sleep
is racked by dreams. They wake crying of war.
Pushing a pram in 1961,
I remember how love weighed, anger shored
against helplessness, how we wrote letters
to the papers, raged at Strontium 90,
the bitter rain that stained our mother-milk.

Yet my daughter's beautiful,
and my daughter's daughter, even then printed
in the womb of the waking embryo,
now resolves into her elements.
Shadow on shining, here she comes dancing
through the bright window of ultra-sound,
fiercer than death and kicking to be born.

In times like these we should praise trees and babies
and take the children walking in beech-woods.

Ballad of Lumb Mill
which made nothing but black silk for widows

The Colden's a winding, slapping sheet
in the storm of grief, the wind and the sleet.

Nothing but endless black silk in their hands
slithers like water-snakes, death on their minds.

Water is dark in its warp and its woof.
Webs hang in swathes from the wheel-house roof.

Clogs on the cobbles, metal on stone,
labour-worn bodies pared to the bone.

Burning mill-chimneys blow smouldering ash
drifting the valley, smutting the wash.

The stain of the dye in the bubbling vats
is colour of shadows, colour of rats.

Looms drum like heartbeats, the river runs black,
delicate threads of the moth and the bat.

Fingers are cold with nothing but cloth,
oil-slick on water. The bat and the moth

measuring darkness, measuring light,
burning their wings in perpetual night.

In Colden's long water the flickering gleam
is glint of the shuttle, trout in a stream.

Reflections go running, wriggle of eels,
shimmers in taffeta, oil in the wheels.

Texture of gros grain, cold petticoats,
buttoned-up bodices stiff at the throat.

Not crêpe-de-Chine chiffon the colour of air,
his hands on her skin, his face in her hair,

but heavy as misery, cold as the stones,
silk to wrap shadows about her old bones.

Water is dark in its warp and its weft,
derelict chimneys all that is left.

Under the shadow of branch and of leaf
the Colden is colder and blacker than grief.

Slate Mine

Into the dark out of June heat,
under the forest's root, past Private,
Danger, Forbidden, past wheels, pulleys,
chains stilled in their pollens of rust.

We stoop through its porch,
to the knees in ice. Torchlight flutters
on wet stone and dies at the brink
of the first gallery.

In the next, and the next, emptiness deep
as cathedrals, then one where a stream hangs
three hundred feet in glittering stillness
and ferns lean to drink at sunlight.

Rungs crook rusted fingers over the drop,
the miner's footprint in air, his hand-print
on rockface and roofscape slimed
by a century of rain.

My cast slate panics
through generations of silence,
such a long wait
for the sound of drowning.

Roofing

Is it the regularity of slate
or thought of the body safe in its den
that makes the raising of the roof so right?

Somewhere for drumming knucklebones of rain
in the rattled nervousness of night,
or shawls of January snow thrown

over a domestic geometry.
Last day of the year. The hammer taps,
setting the courses against winter sky.

Neat as a darn they lap and overlap.
With frozen hands we put the tools away.
The afternoon has lapsed. Dusk mends the gap

with slate-dark purples, and where the holes are
the risen wind comes in, and the first star.

Slate

Lifting the slab takes our breath away
Corner to edge, edge to corner.
Its weight steps the plank
shifting from foot to foot.

The van groans slowly home.
We pause to think, eye the gap
and heave again.
A quarter of a ton.

What weighs is the power of it
trembling at finger-tip,
its balancing moment
held like feathers.

Grindings pressed to slate
electric in my hands. We lean
on the ropes and let it
slowly into fresh cement.

Its purples multiplied
as snows, rains, rivers
that laid themselves down
too finely to see or count,

as many stone-years as wings
of the heath blue, jay feather, layers
of oak-shadow, beechmast,
print of a mountain-ash on rockface.

The tree in the crevice, quarryman
in the glittering slip of rain
on million-faceted blue Blaenau,
the purples of Penrhyn.

So the dairy slab that cooled
junkets and wheys, wide dishes of milk
beading with cream, skims for churning,
now becomes pentanfaen,

hearthstone. Milky planets
trapped in its sheets
when the book was printed,
float in the slate,

water-marked pages
under a stove's feet.

Pipistrelle

Dusk unwinds its spool
among the stems of plum-trees.
Subliminal messenger
on the screen of evening.
A night-glance as day cools
on the house-walls.

We love what we can't see,
illegible freehand
fills every inch of the page.
We sit after midnight
till the ashes cool
and the bottle's empty.

This one, in a box, mouse
the size of my thumb in its furs
and sepia webs of silk
a small foreboding,
the psalms of its veins
on bible-paper,

like a rose I spread once in a book
till you could read your future
in the fine print.

Fulmarus Glacialis

for Christine Evans

Filing the fulmar you post me from Llŷn
I turn to the bird-book and the cliffs.

Found first in Iceland, 1750,
glacial bird whose wings of snow
throw images of angels on the sea
or a gutfull of stinking oil in the enemy's face.

Pilgrim. Discoverer. On the bird-map
Britain's little island's coiffed
with foam of fulmar.
Once rare visitor, she takes the coast.

Between small-print of shore
and broad stroke of the littoral
is fulmar territory, Rockall to Fastnet,
Lundy to Hebrides.

In seabird's slow increase she drew the map
in feathery sea-script, set her single egg
on the palm of every ledge
till that first visitor became a million birds.

Bridle the fulmar. Borrow the lover's llatai
for carrying a message to a friend
a hundred miles or so across the Bay
down the bright water-lines, Ceredigion to Llŷn.

Racing Pigeon

Sunburst of angel
from the dark of a thornbush.
The spaniel makes a dash for it
and has to be held back.

It struts in its anklets
ruffling on the high wall,
storm-blown from the sea,
charts erased from its brain.

It suns itself on warm stone
and takes our hospitality,
a dish of sunflower seeds,
a bowl of rainwater.

Day after day it inclines less
to the lost road of the air,
tries a small circle on blue,
cannot find the thread of wind that brought it.

Somewhere the track ran out under its wings.
There's something we try to remember,
like conscience
at the edge of the mind.

I try again to read its bracelets
but before I'm sure it turns
on rose-quartz toes,
its eye a ring of fire.

Sun runs a finger
over its collar of opals.
Wind stirs the cirrus of its throat,
taking its time.

Magpie in Snow

Etched where it flew
under the garden table, twice
breasting the drift, spread feathers
of flight cut in the snow's glass,

two fingerprints
in Leonardo's sketchbooks
where grain and force of waves
are held in ice. Magpies

skim snow at the speed of hunger
and snow like memory or rock
remembers. Here's the whirr
of wings in your ear and a sob

of frozen air. At daybreak
while we slept it left its image
in the mirror, filled the shallows
with a rinse of palest blue.

Tawny Owl

Plain song of owl
moonlight between cruciform
shadows of hunting.

She sings again
closer
in the sycamore,

her coming quieter
than the wash
behind the wave,

her absence darker
than privacy
in the leaves' tabernacle.

Compline. Vigil.
Stations of the dark.
A flame floats on oil

in her amber eye.
Shoulderless shadow
nightwatching.

Kyrie. Kyrie.

Peregrine Falcon

New blood in the killing-ground,
her scullery,
her boneyard.

I touch the raw wire
of vertigo
feet from the edge.

Her house is air. She comes downstairs
on a turn of wind.
This is her table.

She is arrow.
At two miles a minute
the pigeon bursts like a city.

While we turned our backs
she wasted nothing
but a rose-ringed foot

still warm.

Clocks
for Cai

We walk the lanes to pick them.
'Ffwff-ffwffs'. He gives them the name
he gives to all flowers. 'Ffwff! Ffwff!'
I teach him to tell the time
by dandelion. 'One o' clock. Two.'
He blows me a field of gold
from the palm of his hand
and learns the power of naming.

The sun goes down in the sea
and the moon's translucent.
He's wary of waves and sand's
soft treachery underfoot.
'What does the sea say?' I ask.
'Ffwff! Ffwff!' he answers, then turns
his face to the sky and points
to the full-blown moon.

Cofiant

Cofiant means biography. In Wales the tradition of the *Cofiant* developed in the nineteenth century when many hundreds were written, mainly about preachers. They usually included an account of the subject's life, a selection of his sermons, letters and other writings and ended with tributes and an elegy.

In this poem I refer to *Cofiant a Phregethau y Parch. Thomas Williams, Llangynog*. It was written by his eldest son, and the eldest of his nineteen children, my father's namesake, John Penri Williams, and was printed in 1887. Thomas Williams was my great-great grandfather.

Quotations from the above *Cofiant* and from the *Chronicles of the Princes* are translated from Welsh. I refer also to *The Genealogies of Gwynedd* by J.E. Griffith.

Houses we've lived in
inhabit us
and history's restless
in the rooms of the mind.

*

We took a flat in the family house.
Years later the old neighbour opposite
owned that, watching our arrival, she had said
'Children have come to live at Number One.'

The rooms were tall and hollow. Sun
printed the boards with parallelograms.
Between stained borders floors showed ghosts
of carpets that belonged to someone else.

Nothing had changed since 1926.
'First house on the meadow', a neighbour said.
'Pheasants used to perch there on your gate.'
My widowed grandmother and her daughters

refugees who'd happened to escape
the hungry farms they'd left. Her son
had gone to sea, the desolation
of the coal-fields missed by chance.

*

We came in March and month by month eight windows
that began with rain filled up with aspen leaves
as April became May and nothing was
but bluebells filling rooms with scent of blue.

*

How can you leave a house?
Do they know, who live there,
how I tread the loose tile in the hall,
feel for the light the wrong side of the door,
add my prints to their prints to my old prints
on the finger-plate?

How, at this very second,
I am crossing the room?

*

Apart from one lit, introspective square,
seventeen black windows watch the rain.
Three chimneys swallow the wind.
In the green room the gas fire wavers
as the wind breathes in.

In the brown room the piano is silent.
In another the sockets are emptied
of deck, amplifier, keyboard, guitar.
Blue-tack pegs the empty poster squares
as pegs left out to green on the garden line.
There are no damp towels on the carpet,
no paint drying or gaudy disorder
or books folded back for reading.

The front door shifts in its frame.
No-one slams it. The last bus comes and goes.

Two sons were born in this bed,
their sister asleep in a neighbouring room.
Dam-burst in the pit of the pelvis,
belly-blow of sea in a hidden cave.
The blaze whitened my mind,
my heart clenched its fist of blood.
No wonder they speak of stars
and storms in heaven.

*

'And it was the six hundred and ninetieth year of Christ.
And the milk and butter were changed to blood.
And the moon changed to the colour of blood.'

*

Blaen Cwrt, longhouse,
stepping-stone for the west wind's foot.
Colby, called Number One
with its pebble-dash symmetry.

Ship-shaped Flatholm of the island name.
Bryn Isaf on the hill
above the weed-blurred railway line.
Ceryg-yr-Wyn where the clergyman's
nineteen children were born.
A new Cae Coch on the crossroads
beside the ruined birthplace.
Crugan, four-square farm in slate and stone
in acres of good land.
Bachellyn derelict, where the brother lived.
Broom Hall, the rich son's house of treasure
with Werglodd Fawr in ruins under its feet.
Hendrewen and Chwilog, old lost farms
and nameless hovels, halls and castles
of the far-off dead long fallen to ruin.

                              *

                    Gruffydd (1047)

'And then about seven-score men
of Gruffydd's tribe
died through the treachery
of the men of Ystrad Tywi.
And to avenge his men
Gruffydd ravaged Dyfed and Ystrad Tywi.
And there came a great snow
on the Calends of January
and it lasted until the Feast of Patrick.'

                              *

Wind felled the poplar
with an axe of air.

Its roots tilted a shield
of fibrous mould.

All day we worked in the cold sun,
bill-hook, chainsaw and axe crossing the grain.

Broken ripples, annular rings
counting the generations.

*

Their midsummer wedding
a year before my birth.
Wasn't I there, in the June heat?
I call back breath of roses,
fields of cut hay over a chapel wall.
A perfect day for harvest.
My mother's brothers itch in borrowed clothes
sniffing the air for rain,
running a finger underneath stiff collars.
Black curls spring from combed water,
eyes clear as summer
under the thunder of the brows.

A festival in my mind
or funeral I have mixed with roses
in the album's tinted photographs.

*

John Penri Williams (1899-1957) ‑ *father*

In the margins of books, poems printed
on foxed, bevelled pages; under the shelf
where we peeled back the old wallpaper;
lists; old letters; diaries; notebooks;
copperplate in blacklead and washable Quink,
the Conway Stewart with a golden lever
and its intake of sound as the ink-sac swelled;
commentary; schedules; signatures.
How, after thirty years, do I know his hand?

Chapel boy from Carmarthenshire
locked in his cabin, writing home,
'Annwyl Mam,' shocked by crew-talk,
or tapping morse as the world burned.
He drummed bad news on the sea's skin,
his air-waves singing over the roof
of the whale's auditorium. Only his heart,
the coded pulse over dark water
to a listening ship and the girl at home.

68

Twenty years away his daughter waits
to knock him dizzy with her birth
and scarcely twenty more
he'll strike her silent with his death,
going out on a rainy evening
in May when she isn't looking,
with a 'Hwyl fawr, Cariad.'
No message. Just, 'Over'.

*

An over-turned wine-glass
in wet grass,
one sip like guilt
in the spoon of the tongue.

The fire's dissolved
to bird-bones.
A small lake shivers
in the deck-chair's lap.

*

Phyllis (1895-1985)

Nearly ninety, leaning on my arm,
taking me down the road on her usual walk,
my aunt, his sister, stopped at the iron railings.
We looked down on the flood-plain of the Tywi
from where steep ground brought the town to a sudden halt.
Old settlements, broken things showing their bones,
the Roman 'caer' branded on the town's name,
the medieval church, the Civil War,
and down there the unmistakable straight line
between trees and scrub and bramble hedges:
'The Aberystwyth train', she said, seeing a puff
of steam, hearing the shunt of its struggle
out of the distant station.

All the way to the sea
you can still see where it went
over and under the roads, like someone blind
who remembers the way and steps out straight
through a creeping cataract of moss and bramble.

69

Now that she's dead when I recall her voice
she is musing to herself, 'the Aberystwyth train'.

*

Wil Williams (1861-1910)

He kept a garden
like other railwaymen
in that old world of the Great Western.
When his daughter went back
It disappointed her.
How sad, she said,
to see my mother's house so shabby,
the yard-hens scraggy,
the stackyard sour with old hay,
the house dirty.

I can't see the house in her mind,
only the white farm on the hill
that is still there.
Down through the tunnels along the line
they run away from us,
the rooms, the women who tended them,
the dressers of glinting jugs,
the lines of sweet washing between trees.
The stations with their cabbage-patches
and tubbed geraniums are closed
and the trains' long cries are swallowed
in the throats of tunnels.

*

Orchis Mascula

Hot stink of orchid in the woods at Fforest.
Downstream of the waterfall I breathed
their scent and touched their purple towers,
the swollen root that cures the King's Evil
and makes the heart hot. Not flowers to share
to bring home for a jar.
Ophelia's long purples, tragic flowers.
You could believe they grew beneath the cross

and no amount of rain could wash the blood
from their stained leaves.

They called and called but I would not hear,
mixing their voices with waves and water.
Crouched in the blackthorn tunnel the cattle made
as they swayed their way to the sea, loosed
from the beudy by Gwilym and slapped free,
I was hooked on dens and secret places,
illicit books, visions and diaries
and the tomcat stink of orchids. Nothing
would fetch me out but hunger, or the sound
of shadows stepping closer.

*

Annie (1868-1944)

I called her Ga, and a child's stuttered
syllable became her name.
A widow nearly forty years,
beautiful and straight-backed,
always with a bit of lace about her,
pearls the colour of her twisted hair,
the scent of lavender.

It was our job at Fforest to feed the hens
with cool and liquid handfuls of thrown corn.
We looked for eggs smuggled in hedge and hay,
and walked together the narrow path to the sea
calling the seals by their secret names.

At Christmas she rustled packages under her bed
where the po was kept and dusty suitcases.
That year I got an old doll with a china face,
ink-dark eyes and joints at elbows and knees.
Inside her skull, like a tea-pot, under her hair,
beneath her fontanelle, was the cold cave
where her eye-wires rocked her to sleep.

Somewhere in a high hospital window –
I drive past it sometimes with a start of loss –
her pale face made an oval in the glass
over a blue dressing-gown. She waved to me,

too far away to be certain it was her.
They wouldn't let children in.
Then she was lost or somebody gave her away.

*

First spring day in the hills.
Hens laid wild in stack and hedge.
In my palm the ice-egg
was stupidly heavy and still.

Crude pot-egg, overblown acorn
colour of bone, of fungi,
of old stone bottles,
a stone to crack a jaw.

Not delicate
like Nain's china eggs,
crazed little stone skulls,
false pregnancy, fool's gold.

Easily fooled the old hen
panicked to quicken it
under her breast-down. Stone
under the heart, stillborn.

*

Thomas Williams (1800-1885)

Child of Christmas and the turning century,
born to holy bells and the tolling sea,
he carried two voices into manhood:
the call of the sea and the call of God.

He writes how he'd never known a time
when longing for sea's rhythm
underfoot and the hot rope in his hands
reining an apron of sail as he held the wind,

was not a stinging fire in his mind,
or when the tug of religion started
turning his heart into the gale.
He took lodgings in Pwllheli and set sail.

72

The boat carried limestone across the Straits,
Môn to Caernarfon. He set his sights
on the torn coastline, crossing the grain
of knotty currents, westerlies and rain.

*

He was baptised in the stream at Tyddyn Shôn.
I found the place one summer afternoon
where water twisted, as it must have done,
under the bridge in a pool deep enough for a man
to drown his devils in a mountain stream,
leaving his soul caught like a rag on a stone.

*

Ceryg-yr-Wyn (1845)

Near Christmas and the afternoon
already dark. In the yard I could hear Mary
calling the hens.

The little ones ran in and out
of the open door, their clogs
clacking on stone, till there,

a hand away on the hearth
my baby stood lifting his sleeves of fire
like a small angel of annunciation,

his laugh surprised to silence
till he fell burning into my smothering arms.
He never ran again and after three days died.

So quick the moth-wings flared
as they have done
every day since for forty years.

*

'It was the first time grief touched my family, and I have never
felt greater sorrow at the death of anyone until this day.'

*

73

Dear Son,

Your dear mother died at 9 o'clock today and the burial has been arranged for 2 o'clock on Friday. The doctor said her main affliction was maternal tenderness, grief for Peter, and watching her other children lying sick and she unable to help them. I think Janet is a little better, but Samuel and the other children are still very ill.

Your grieving father,
Thomas Williams

*

Jennet (1760-1830)

Widow and widower in neighbourly grief.
She married Thomas and went to live with him
at the smallholding on the crossroads.

*

Saint Beuno's, full of breath of the sea, half
choked in elder, the wind's hymn
sings in the thorn. The monks' old

garden fends off the devil with a grove of ash.
Fruit bushes and a tangled hop-vine,
a little pasture to the lee of the wall

show how they survived against the wash
of Atlantic salt, poverty, chastity, stations
of work and prayer between sea and hill.

Where Jennet stood, to marry or mourn
three husbands or see her son baptised,
how many saints prayed on their way to die

on the holy island? How many fatherless newborn
wailed in their mothers' arms for ships capsized
in the Straits, where their fathers lie?

74

the church is dark for an illiterate
congregation, the lepers' window shadowed
with the living dead, those still forbidden

at our door as we cast the disconsolate
from their proper place, the sick, the doomed
who carry the virus or bacillus we call sin.

*

Under the altar a tall saint lies.
In the oval graveyard her kinsmen's bones
unthread themselves and slip among the stones

with holy relics. I can't find their grave
lost to the rampant daneberry fruited with blood
of fallen Norsemen, flourishing where they died.

*

Broom Hall, formerly Werglodd Fawr, in the parish of Llanarmon
in Caernarfonshire, a late Georgian house in the austere style of
the early nineteenth century, in brick, stucco and slate, with slate-
roofed verandahs, terraces and colonnades.

*

Rowland Jones (1772-1856),
grandson of William Jones of Crugan

Brought up in Hanover Square
in a house of women,
he never married.
When he came of age
he took his fortune home.
They called him 'Mr Jones of London'.

His father burned his eyes and health with study
but the son burnished his with seeing.
He built Broom Hall among the stones

of Werglodd Fawr
and filled its rooms
with art and elegance, setting
lawns and pleasure grounds on his savage acres.

His ancestors laboured on stony farms,
thatched smallholdings, crude halls, embattled castles.
He, a gentleman, spent his life's energy
in overseeing work, a preoccupation
with plans and fine proportions.
His cousins' descendants would again

be labourers and live on smallholdings
and have their lives cut short by poverty,
taking the places of those he oversaw
building his house, setting his straight lines down,
bringing the carriage to the door to meet him
and dying of fevers that swept the poor.

*

On the twenty fourth day of February, eighteen hundred and
fifty seven, for thirteen days, Broom Hall, formerly Werglodd
Fawr, in the parish of Llanarmon in Caernarfonshire, a late Geor-
gian house in the austere style of the early nineteenth century,
in brick stucco and slate with slate-roofed verandahs, terraces
and colonnades. House, grounds and contents: gallery and
cabinet pictures and portraits by Carracci, Domenichino, Rubens,
Teniers, Watteau, Storck, Pater, Holbein et cetera; statuary,
cabinets and tables of Florentine mosaic, ebony and marqueterie;
superb old Dresden and Oriental China; manicure sets and silver
gilt caskets, inkstands and boxes; two costly toilet cases; valuable
jewellery and filigree; eight thousand ounces of silver gilt and
silver plate; excellent household furniture; organs and musical
boxes; library of books and manuscripts; cellar of choice old
wines; two handsome travelling carriages; phaeton, fire engine,
greenhouse plants et cetera.

*

Rowland Jones (1716-1774),
second son of William Jones of Crugan

Second son of the farm, sent to grammar school
at Botwnnog to make a lawyer of him.
Classical languages and arithmetic
were all he'd need. In a pool
of candlelight at his uncle's farm
the clever boy found wonders in his books.
Hearth-Welsh, gentry English, a scholar's Greek and Latin,
shadow-eyed in the smoke of that low room,
he found obsession on the flickering page.
Later, man of letters and law at Symond's Inn,
he studied words known since his mother's womb,
saw in old Celtic all primeval language
broken by the scattering winds of Babel
from the first stuttered monosyllable.

*

A man used to listening,
they say he overheard a confidence
and turned it to advantage.
He married money and Elizabeth,
and turned the fortune home to Eifionydd,
dreaming on Werglodd Fawr of the fine house
his infant son would build over the ruins.

*

His grave, his stone,
his parts of speech all gone
under the city's monotone.

At St James, Piccadilly,
they've tidied the torn pages
of the stones,

so there's no telling now
the body's syllables
or testament of bones.

*

77

'And then there was the Battle of Mechain
between Bleddyn and Rhiwallon,
sons of Cynfyn,
and Meredydd and Ithel,
sons of Gruffydd.
And there the sons of Gruffydd fell.
Ithel was slain in the fight
and Meredydd perished of cold as he fled.
And there Rhiwallon ap Cynfyn was slain.
And then Bleddyn ap Cynfyn
held Gwynedd and Powys,
and Meredydd ab Owain ab Edwin
held Deheubarth.'

*

The sea wastes words
where the tide's fretwork
has worn half the hill-fort away.

It drafts and re-drafts the coast
and is never done
writing at the edge

its doodle of scum,
driftwood, rope and bottles
and skulls of birds.

*

Daughter of Penri Williams, wireless engineer of Carmarthenshire
    and Ceinwen Evans of Denbighshire
son of William Williams, railwayman and Annie of Carmarthenshire
son of Daniel Williams, railwayman of Llangynog and Sara
son of Thomas Williams, Baptist minister and Mary
son of Thomas Williams, smallholder of Nefyn and Jennet of Pystyll
son of William Williams, farmer of Crugan, Llanbedrog
son of William Jones, farmer of Crugan
son of John Williams, farmer and lawyer of Crugan
son of William and Mary
son of Robert and Margaret
son of John and Catherine
son of Robert and Elizabeth
son of Owen of Eifionydd
son of Owain
son of John
son of Meurig of Eifionydd
son of Llewelyn and Margaret Fychan
son of Cynwrig Fychan and Margaret, d. of Rhys ap Siencyn
son of Cynwrig of Llŷn and his nameless wife
son of Madog Fychan and Gwenllian, d. of Ithel Fychan
son of Madog Crupl and Margaret, d. of Rhys Fychan
son of Gruffydd, Barŵn Gwyn of Glyndyfrdwy and Margaret
son of Gruffydd, Lord of Dinas Brân and Emma Audley
son of Madog of Powys and Ysola d. of Ithel
son of Gruffydd Maelor of Powys and Angharad, d. of Owain
    Gwynedd
son of Madog of Powys and Susannah d. of Gruffydd ap Cynan
son of Meredydd of Powys and Hunydd, d. of Eunydd ap
    Gwerngwy
son of Bleddyn of Powys and Haer, d. of Cyllin ap y Blaidd
    Rhydd
son of Cynfyn and Angharad
son of Gwerystan and Nest
son of Gwaethfoed of Cibwr in Gwent and Morfudd, d. of Ynyr
    Ddu

*